Printed in the United States of America

ISBN-13: 978-1492848707

ISBN-10: 1492848700

Edited by D.J. Natelson

Responsive Web Design
Overview For Beginners

Preface

This book provides an overview of responsive web design for those who are not familiar with the topic.

This book is not meant to show how a responsive web design is implemented. It is meant to provide enough background to allow someone currently unfamiliar with the topic to understand the need for responsive web design and its associated cost.

Included are some very light examples of responsive web design implementation. These are enough to whet the technical appetite but shouldn't bog down a beginner in technical minutia.

Feel free to contact me anytime through my website at www.bitesizebschool.com.

Special Offer

The last chapter of this book presents a generous special offer for those wanting to go beyond the basics and take full command of responsive web design.

Even if you decide not to take advantage of this great opportunity, I hope you enjoy the book and walk away with a better understanding of responsive web design.

Chapter 1

Responsive Web Design Overview

A responsive web design allows your website to be viewed across multiple screen sizes while maintaining its integrity. This means that as a user's screen width decreases, your website doesn't shrink. It remains readable and usable.

To allow for readability and usability, a responsive web design website will rearrange some items while maintaining a consistent look. For example, the sidebar might disappear, or the navigation menu may flip from horizontal to vertical.

These rearrangements usually happen at certain screen widths and not all at once. If there is not enough room for the sidebar at 450-pixel width, for example, the sidebar will disappear. This prevents horizontal scrolling, which responsive web designs do not have.

The absence of horizontal scrolling is a critical component of a responsive web design. Users of a responsive web design-enabled site should be able to do everything on the website with only vertical scrolling.

While responsive web design allows the user to get a rich experience, even at smaller screen sizes, it doesn't guarantee that all desktop functionality is available at smaller screen sizes. A responsive web design tries to provide readability and usability along with core functionality, but not necessarily full functionality.

Core functionality means that some of your website's functionality may not be available on a smaller screen or mobile device. For example, Java-, Javascript-, or Silverlight-dependent functionality may not be available on smaller screens. Usually, the absence of this functionality will not compromise the website.

Responsive web designs are not limited to smaller screens. They work in both directions (i.e., also on larger screens). But the majority of responsive web design focuses on smaller screens, which is what this book will focus on.

Chapter 2

Usability of Smaller Screens

When you design a responsive web design, you will eventually get the site working on smaller and smaller screens. But simply getting the site usable at smaller screens may not be enough.

What do I mean by that? A little more work is involved in presenting a superior user experience than simply making sites look great on smaller screens.

For example:

1. The text might be too small.
2. The navigation menu items may be too close together for a user to tap a single item quickly with a finger.
3. Some of the most important data that was at the top of your site on the desktop version may now be

in the middle or at the bottom,
necessitating a lot of scrolling.

Smaller mobile devices are about
extreme efficiency and speed. Users are
likely to be on the go and want relevant
information quickly. Unlike desktop
screens, where the users are sitting
down and have time to focus on content
and absorb what it means, small device
users need information swiftly — which
makes websites not designed with
optimal mobile experiences in mind
difficult and frustrating environments
for mobile users.

Users might be standing in a
shopping line holding their phones with
one hand. They don't have time to
fumble around trying to click a super
tiny link, or tackle the tedious task of
pinching and zooming because the text
is so small.

Thoroughly test your website at
smaller screens, giving it a workout in
the real world. Get into situations your

users will probably find themselves in. With smaller screens, does your site lend itself to enabling users or hindering them?

Responsive web design creates consistent experiences as you go from desktop, to tablet, to mobile.

Users don't expect the same experience on their mobile devices as they do on the desktop, but they do expect a consistent, quality experience at smaller screens. Make them happy and you'll keep your users coming back for more.

Chapter 3

Why Plugins Aren't the Solution

Properly implementing a responsive web design takes some rethinking about how you want to display your website content. Transformations occur as screen size gets smaller, ultimately culminating into a single column.

If you're used to thinking in two columns (main content plus side bar) or even three (as in a newspaper layout), figuring out how to transform down to one column takes a realignment in your thinking.

Some WordPress plugins do attempt to get websites into a presentable form for mobile users. However, many plugins tend to mangle your site. Without some thorough confirmation of what pages actually look like, you might initially get the impression that everything is okay. A word of caution: Be sure to give your site a thorough check after installing a mobile-related plugins.

Another drawback of plugins is they aren't consistent with your site's layout. This gives your website the appearance of two different sites. It isn't uncommon for a mobile website to look different from the full-blown desktop version. However, this a mistake, as it degrades its brand.

A responsive web design allows you to peel away some of the layers of your brand as you move your website's content into one column. But peeling away layers is not the same as presenting a completely different look.

Brands often present themselves differently in different contexts. The Apple logo on the lid of my MacBook Pro is smoky white and lights up. At WDC (the developers conference where Apple usually shows off upcoming products), the logo can be many different colors with lots of interesting detail . . . but the consistent logo outline is still very visible.

The abstract element of our business we call "brand" is very fragile. Lots of work is required to continue building it and ensure no harm comes to it.

Designing your site with a responsive web design in mind, rather than handing everything off to a plugin, can help ensure your brand remains healthy and consistent.

Chapter 4

Why a Responsive Web Design Theme May Not Be Best for Your Existing Website

You've poured a lot of effort and time in getting your website to where it's at—including custom CSS, widgets, theme modifications, and maybe even custom PHP. But all of those changes are likely to get wiped out if you slap on a new theme.

To say the least, it's a perilous situation. Maybe akin to playing Russian roulette.

Before attempting to apply any theme, whether to back up your website shouldn't even be a question. You do have a backup system in place, right?

But if the theme doesn't work out, and you find too much of your custom functionality is lost, getting your backup restored can easily turn into a mangled mess. In the meantime, your website might only be partially available or, worse, completely down.

There's a way to get a responsive web design without having to apply a new theme. If you already have CSS and HTML skills, applying a responsive web design will be like learning a new web design technique.

By going the do-it-yourself route, you'll also have complete control. Some themes may do what you want initially, but then you find they have limitations. Trying to modify the theme can become a big pain.

But if the code is yours from the beginning, you'll understand and know what is going on. This makes any changes much easier.

Chapter 5

Risks Involved with Responsive Web Design Frameworks

Believe it or not, responsive web design is still in its early days. There aren't any official standards on how it should work. But then again, there aren't any official standards on how a mobile site should work.

And therein lies the risk of using any responsive web design framework. It might sound like a good idea to use such a framework. After all, you're likely to see some quick payoff . . . at least if you are designing a new website. For an existing site, it could be more work than it's worth.

The bigger problem is, since we are still in the early days of what responsive web design means, responsive web design frameworks will change and evolve. Some will probably even go away.

If you integrate a framework and, a few months later, the creator decides it is too much work to continue it and pulls all support and future updates, you're stuck with a doorstop. Now it is up to you to keep your website up to date in addition to dealing with an obsolete framework. That's a little too much for most small companies.

If you're not going to use a framework, what are the other options? Stay loose and independent. What does that mean, exactly?

Responsive web design is likely to be composed of CSS (CSS3, to be exact) for the foreseeable future. CSS isn't going anywhere. Sticking to the core components of responsive web design will ensure you don't have any tight integration or exposure to framework that might render you unable to make use of the latest responsive design techniques.

Since its inception in 2010, not much has evolved in the core components of responsive web design. What worked in 2010 works just fine today. What has come along is the large number of responsive web design templates.

Until responsive design is built into browsers, rolling your own will pay big dividends in scaleability and maintainability.

Chapter 6

**Responsive Web Design or Mobile
Website: Which Is Right for You?**

It's not uncommon to see the term
"responsive web design" used
interchangeably with the term "mobile
website." On the surface, they look very
similar. However, the two are very
different.

Responsive Web Design

First, let's look at responsive web
design. This type of website scales
fluidly as the screen size changes. The
website mostly keeps its original look,
providing consistency across different
screen sizes.

A responsive web design
accomplishes its scaling using CSS.
Specifically, media queries (a
component of CSS) are a core part of a
responsive web design.

A responsive web design is not concerned with devices. It is instead concerned with screen size.

A Mobile Website

On the other hand, a mobile website is looking for specific device types. Once any number of target device types is found, a completely different website is served up.

By a different website, I mean a website that has been designed specifically for mobile devices. Instead of a URL such as www.mywebsite.com, the URL might look like m.mywebsite.com.

Since a mobile website is basically built from the ground up for mobile devices, it can offer functionality specifically targeted for mobile devices. This is in contrast to a responsive web design, which is more generic and may not be as flexible on mobile devices, and therefore may have limited functionality.

A mobile website may display only a map, phone number, and hours — just the items that mobile users need while they are on the go.

A mobile website might provide functionality that is different from the desktop version of the site. For example, it might utilize a accelerometer or gyroscope.

Conclusion

While a responsive web design and mobile website may be used interchangeably, you can see they have different purposes and are, in fact, different under the hood.

Chapter 7

Measuring the Cost of a Responsive Web Design

Building a website from scratch is a great cost benefit of responsive web design. It is less complex to implement a responsive web design on a new site than an old one.

But more often than not, we are dealing with an existing, complex website. One that likely has a heavily modified theme. This means we can't replace the theme. We are basically married to it going forward. The cost of replacing the theme and all the work that went into it would be substantial.

In this case, the cost of creating a new responsive design website vs. implementing it into our existing site needs to be measured.

In considering cost associated with a new site (assuming you want very similar functionality that is probably not available in any stock theme), we need to recognize that we are not only rebuilding existing functionality, we are also implementing a responsive design.

In most cases, the cost associated with rebuilding existing functionality will be higher than the responsive design cost.

Depending on the theme chosen, existing functionality will be difficult to port over. This difficulty greatly increases if you go with a completely new framework. In that regard, I don't think a new framework adds much additional time (except that of learning how to use the new framework).

When implementing a responsive web design into an existing site, much of the existing functionality can be saved—a great cost reduction.

Because the responsive web design is a different architecture than that of the current theme, this is where our cost will be focused. Think of it like retrofitting an old English building with modern wiring. It can be a lot of work, but how much really depends on how the building was built.

The more fixed widths and non-specific heights of elements, the more difficult it will be to implement a responsive web design. But that is the starting point.

Some areas of the site won't be fixed with just a 100% width and height specification on elements. These areas will require new thinking and design.

In summary: The more complex and large your site, the more savings will be realized when you implement a responsive web design instead of building and maintaining a mobile version.

Chapter 8

Designer's View on Cost

I want to demonstrate to you how a designer might view estimating a responsive web design project. Understanding this allows business owners to see the considerations a designer has to take into account. Furthermore, being able to see both sides of the bargaining table can lead to a more satisfactory relationship between client and designer.

As a designer, if you're new to responsive web design (RWD), putting together an accurate bid for your first RWD project can be scary. There are many unknowns with which to contend.

For your first project, it might be safest to go with hourly billing. Once you have a few projects under your belt, you can switch to higher-priced project-based billing.

To make your RWD projects go more smoothly, constantly educate your clients about RWD. This will help get the clients involved, allow them to understand your decisions, and how they impact their sites.

In fact, educating your clients should be a big part of your RWD client process. Not just because many clients aren't intimately familiar with RWD, but also because it is still relatively new.

If you can build trust at this stage, there's a good chance you'll end up having the client see you as the go-to web designer.

We already know there will be unknowns on the project, but how do we cope with them financially? Certainly, we want to be correctly compensated for our time.

There are parts of the project that should be fairly known. We can apply our hourly rate to those. This gives us some guaranteed value on fairly known areas. Now we must get into the detailed work of providing some estimate around the unknowns.

Rather than trying to focus on small, unknown pieces, begin by identifying large boxes — large areas of work that are unknowns but related. The big related area can be put into a box. Give each box a description.

Once you've identified all the unknown boxes, you can start putting together some type of workflow within the box — meaning you can begin identifying smaller boxes within a box.

For some of these smaller boxes, you just won't know how exactly much time is involved, but you should have some vague idea. Apply your estimate using days. This allows for a lot of padding.

Add up all the time in your smaller boxes. This will provide an estimate for the larger parent box. Now you're starting to get some estimate around the unknowns. You can add this to your already known estimate, which is based on hours.

You might decide to add or subtract time from your new total estimate, depending on how realistic you feel it is. At least at this point, you aren't just swinging at anything in the wind. You have a fairly analytical basis for your estimate.

Chapter 9

Handling Ads in Your Responsive Web Design

When setting up an ad campaign, you usually configure the ad dimensions based on the desktop version of your website. But what happens at smaller screen widths when your responsive design kicks in?

If the ads are in your sidebar, they may just tag along with your sidebar. If you hide the sidebar at lower widths, the ads will be hidden. But if you stack the sidebar under other content, the ads might be too wide for the screen width. At this point, a decision needs to be made about reformatting or perhaps removing the ads altogether.

Let's consider the first scenario — reformatting the ads. Depending on the agreement you have with each respective ad network, reformatting or resizing the ads may not be an option.

If reformatting is not an option, check with the ad network for an optional size. Be clear you are displaying only one instance of that ad at a time—meaning the full desktop ad will be hidden when the smaller ad displays.

The next option is to reformat the ad to a different size. This may require rewriting your copy. Whether it does will depend on how much space you're going to allow for the ad. On a mobile device, an ad consuming lots of vertical space won't provide for a pleasant user experience.

You might decide not to display the ad but still show sidebar content. In that case, you can wrap the ad in a div and give the div a name. Next, find a width range in which the ad will not work. Target the ad's div (through the name we provided for the div) by hiding it.

There is a balance you'll need to weigh between ad network restrictions and user experience vs. revenue. The above are a few important factors to consider when displaying any ads on smaller screens.

Chapter 10

Responsive Email

If you're not already using an email format that looks great on mobile devices, this is an area that you might want to start with before transforming your website into a responsive web design.

It's quicker and easier to make your emails look great on mobile devices vs. your website. You should also reap immediate dividends in that more people will be able and probably want to read your emails on their mobile devices.

Announcing your new email format on your website and explaining why you've gone responsive is sure to draw more interest with your existing email subscribers.

Since this book isn't technically heavy, we'll look at how to easily create a great looking email on mobile devices.

Mobile Email Formatting The Easy Way

Most email providers follow similar workflows for creating a campaign. The general steps I outline here should work with your email provider. Of course, you can always check with your email provider to help you fill in any details but at least now you'll have the necessary knowledge.

An email campaign is simply an email you send out to your list. It consists of creating the subject, body content, HTML/Text formats and a few other things.

To create a great looking mobile email, we don't need to edit HTML and add media queries. Using a simple plain text format will get the job done fine and will be readable on most any device.

Leaving out HTML and going with plain text means more devices can easily format your email. It also means the probably of successfully getting through spam filters increases (we're more likely to reach our readers).

You're probably wondering how are plain text emails created? Check with your email provider for the exact template name, but it should be named something similar to "plain text email".

That is the template to use that should look great on mobile devices and desktops alike.

The Problems Of Fixed Width

Fixed width in email can be a big problem but we're going to see how to avoid it. You'll want your text to wrap once it reaches the maximum width of any device.

If your text doesn't wrap, you'll create a fixed width, in which the user will need to scroll horizontally. This doesn't create a pleasing experience for your readers. It's difficult to read emails in which you must keep scrolling horizontally left and right.

Try a test email to your mobile device with the plain text template. You'll want lots of text to see how well it wraps and if there is any fixed width.

If you discover text is not wrapping and you have to scroll horizontally, check with you email provider on how to eliminate fixed width and make text wrap.

As a tip for better readability, I'd suggest using short sentences separated by blank lines. It is usually easier to read text on a computer screen or mobile device when blank lines separate each paragraph.

You want to do all you can to make your reader's experience a great one, especially on mobile devices.

Font Size

Larger fonts are better than smaller fonts when it comes to reading emails on mobile devices. Of course, there is a max font size but it is better to go larger than smaller.

With larger fonts, readers don't have to zoom in to read your content. That is the main reason to use larger fonts.

Theory vs. Practice

Once your plain text email is ready, don't forget to test, especially if this is your first time using the plain text format.

What do your emails look like on your mobile device? Can you have a friend with a different mobile device verify as well?

Once initial testing is complete, you can then reuse your template in future campaigns with reassurance that it will look great across most mobile devices.

It is good discipline to always send a test email to your inbox before publishing any campaign. Even with a high probability that the email will look great, a test email is a good final check and verification.

One Column

Plain text emails imply that content will use one column. One column means each line of text will fill the width of the device without interruption.

By contrast, many websites use at least two columns - one main column for content and a smaller column as a side bar.

Using only one column in a responsive design on smaller screens is a better experience for users, since more text can be displayed and any buttons are large enough to be easily clicked.

While we aren't designing a fully responsive web design email, we are still making it responsive to provide the best mobile experience.

Ads And Responsive Email

In Chapter 9, we looked at using ads on a responsive website. Some of the main points where to use of one column, in which ads must be stacked vertically with regular content.

By stacking ads vertically with regular content, the flow might look like this:

[…text…]
[….ad….]
[…text…]

In the above example, the user reads through our content and then comes across an ad. They can scroll past the ad and continue with the content. There is an even flow and only a minor disruption from the ad. However, the ad does not stop any functionality.

A wide ad format, one that consumes the width of the device is better than a very tall ad. With a tall ad, there is more of a disruption to the user. There is a longer break in reading and the user has to scroll much further before being able to continue reading.

With a wide ad that is not too tall, the advertiser's point can still be made without degrading the user's experience.

In Summary

We've looked at how to make a responsive email. While not fully a responsive web design, plain text emails still do a very good job and provide a great user experience.

Plain text emails are also easy to create, have higher success in getting past spam filters and retain their visual integrity on a large number of devices.

Chapter 11

Responsive Web Design and CSS

Now we shift more into the technical aspects of responsive web design. From here on, you'll get a light introduction into the code behind a responsive web design.

CSS is a core component of a responsive web design. Without CSS, you wouldn't be able to create a responsive web design website.

Particularly, media queries were introduced in CSS3. They allow you to execute code at specific screen sizes. Below is an example of a media query that will change the identifier #mydiv color to black at 500 pixels and under.

```
@media screen and (max-width:500px) {
    #mydiv {color:#000}
}
```

As you can see, this type of conditional media query makes it very easy for your website to adapt to certain screen sizes. Any CSS code that is not inside the media query will execute. Code inside the media query will only execute when the specified condition is met.

You can test media query conditionals by decreasing the width of your desktop web browser. This technique can save time vs. testing against a mobile device, since you'll need to deploy your code to a website for mobile testing — unless you have a local dev site that is accessible.

Besides media queries, CSS is also used to transform different elements. For example, a horizontal navigation changes to a vertical navigation at smaller screen widths.

Sidebars may disappear as well. Removing the sidebar is a matter of hiding its container (usually a div).

Font sizes might increase at smaller screens by applying specific styles. CSS allows you to target nearly any area on your webpage and apply a modification that looks better at a lower screen width.

Chapter 12

HTML5

When reading about responsive web design, you're likely to come across the term HTML5.

HTML5 is the fifth edition of the HTML standard, which is the basic/core markup language for designing webpages.

What does HTML5 have to do with responsive web design? To answer this question, let's do some comparisons.

From chapter 10, we know CSS is needed to create a responsive web design. In particular, CSS3 is needed since it contains media queries. Remember the @media syntax?

HTML is also needed since it is the basic (and sometimes complex) market that helps in creating our webpage layout.

We can now say HTML and CSS are certainly needed to create a responsive web design.

But is there a need for HTML5? Isn't it HTML? Yes. It is HTML. HTML5 introduced new features such as video support, elegant forms, client-side database and more.

Assuming the web browser supports it, all of the previously mentioned HTML5 features are available to you without the need for any plugins or third party components.

But is HTML5 needed for creating responsive web designs? While you will be using HTML to create a responsive website, you don't need to use HTML5 features.

Just like HTML5, CSS3 offers many features that aren't required for a responsive web design. But one feature of CSS3 is required – media queries. Without media queries, we loose the ability to easily target specific CSS to certain screen sizes.

As a side note, javascript is not needed for creating responsive web designs. But it can be used to control certain functionality and visuals. In other words, it's an enhancement. Just like HTML5 features are an enhancement.

To summarize, the core languages we need for a responsive web design are HTML and CSS3. However, we can still use HTML5, javascript and many other languages to enhance our responsive web design.

Chapter 13

5 Steps to a Responsive Web Design

The following are five steps to follow each time you begin implementing a responsive web design, whether it is for a new website or an existing web site.

These steps are:

1. W3C Validation
2. Single Plane
3. Stack It
4. Flexible Grid
5. Awareness

1. W3C Validation

How W3C Validator Works

The W3C Validator identifies any non-confirming code. This helps you to weed out broken code, such as tags missing ending brackets or mismatched divs.

While the validator isn't perfect, it is helpful if you know what to look for and what to ignore.

To use the validator, visit http://validator.w3.org. Enter your website URL. Check the errors section. You can most likely ignore any meta-related entries. Look for entries referencing a missing closing tag or a missing bracket (">").

The validator error description should include a line where the error occurs in your source. If you are using an HTML-type of editor or editing from within WordPress, it may be difficult to figure out where the line number is. You can get the line number by viewing the webpage in a browser.

Next, select "view source" from the browser. Some browsers will place a number next to each line. If you don't see a number to help you identify lines, copy all the source into a text editor that

includes line numbers, such as
NotePad++ (Windows) or TextWrangler
(Mac).

Now that you have identified any
code-related errors, you can fix them in
your editor of choice.

Setting a Baseline

The W3C Validator is meant to save
you time. You want to avoid battling
with your code, trying to fix two divs
overlapping each other, only to finally
realize the issue was a missing closing
div tag.

The W3C Validator is good at
identifying these types of mistakes and
at least starting you off on a fairly stable
baseline . . . from a code-confirming
point of view.

2. Single Plane

Leveling the Playing Field

As you decrease your web browser width, you're likely to find that elements begin overlapping one another. This scenario usually involves DIVs running into one another.

To fix this issue, start by specifying a height for DIVs in the problem area. This will cause other elements to begin reshuffling. You'll start to zero in on which DIVs are causing formatting issues.

"Single plane" refers to removing all overlap and putting divs on the same plane. At this level, divs will push one another over rather than overlap.

Controlling divs that are pushing one another around is much easier than controlling DIVs that are overlapping.

Height with SPAN

SPAN tags aren't block elements. But you may find that by making a SPAN a block element (style="display:block"), the SPAN will

also push other elements around —
assuming you specified a height as well.

Depending on what you are doing
with the SPAN, it might make sense to
switch it out for a DIV, which is a block-
level element.

Moving Code Changes to Media Queries

Once you've identified needed
changes using the above techniques,
begin moving those changes into the
appropriate media queries, allowing the
changes to be enforced only at the
related screen size(s).

Some changes may become part of
your normal style sheet and therefore
not require a media query. For
example, switching a span out for a div,
or specifying the height of an element.
You may want those changes to be
always available.

3. Stack It

Going Vertical

Once basic formatting of your page at lower widths is falling in line and behaving the way you want it to, you'll want to start stacking your page elements into a single column.

It isn't uncommon for a website to use multiple columns. For example, a left or right sidebar and a main content area creates a two-column layout. This two-column layout won't work at lower widths.

Instead, you'll want to stack everything into one vertical column. Here's an example using a horizontal navigation:

Home | Products | Blog | About | Contact Us

. . . transforms to . . .

Home
Products

Blog
About
Contact Us

The horizontal navigation transformed into a vertical navigation.

The sidebar will disappear altogether. You can add a new container DIV that appears only at certain screen widths and holds sidebar content. You probably do not want to display any ads at lower screen widths, depending on their formatting.

The above new DIV will be controlled by media queries. This DIV can go under the main content. The layout might look like this:

[nav]
[main content]
[sidebar content]

4. Flexible Grid

A flexible grid refers to using non-fixed width elements. This means using elements that have a 100% width rather than 500px, for example. At certain screen widths, fixed width is replaced with 100% width in media queries.

Flexible grid can also refer to an adaptive grid. Adaptive grids remain fixed width, but their width reduces at different screen sizes via media queries.

Flexible Images

Images also need to be flexible but usually don't require as much work as grids. By setting image widths to max-width, 100%, images will expand only to their original full width when the screen allows. They will shrink below the original image width as the screen width gets smaller.

Note that max-width does not scale proportionately. While the width will change with the screen size, height will remain the same. This can distort your image, depending on the image's original proportion.

To scale proportionately, combine max-width with height:auto. The following is an example class:

```
.myclass { max-width: 100%; height: auto }
```

You can also use the image slicing technique with certain images. It is more work to slice images, but may be preferable, depending on the consistency and quality you are targeting with images. Depending on your needs, slicing might very well be the best solution for you.

5. Awareness

On The Lookout

Simply being aware of your responsive design can go a long way to maintaining it. This means that, as you create new blog posts or pages, you should be aware of fixed widths and overlapping elements in your code.

If any new HTML is complex, keep in mind you will likely need a media query with some custom CSS to make sure the new code looks nice at different screen widths.

Always check new posts and pages on your mobile device or, at the very least, decrease your browser width. Out of Firefox, Safari, IE, and Chrome, Firefox will provide the smallest width. But it is still good practice to check on an actual device.

Chapter 14

Tips For Modifying Your Live Website

For those that are a one person show, modifying your website usually means working on the site live, while people are visiting it.

This can be a perilous situation. Accidentally breaking the site and bringing it down while people are on it can result in lost sales and credibility with your customers. This is a situation we certainly want to avoid.

Planning your update strategy should be the first step before any modifications begin. This consists of identifying sections to change, understanding the impact, and ordering the changes.

Before we look at the update strategy in more detail, always backup your site before making any changes. This can be a lifesaver. What they say about backups is very true – you don't need them until you do. Add this as a first step to your update plan.

Some type of "under construction" or "we'll be back soon" page should be available to quickly switch over to should anything go wrong. There are a number of Wordpress plugins that will do this. You can search the term "wordpress under construction plugin", which should bring up a variety of such plugins.

Update Strategy

1. The first step in your update strategy is to identify areas you want to change. If you are making changes on the live site, small changes are the best option. Meaning, changes that are isolated. This way, if something goes wrong, it only breaks a small area and shouldn't cascade though out the site.

Plan a time to make changes. Allow for extra time in case anything goes wrong and you need to undo your changes. Have your hosting provider's phone number handy in case the site goes down and you need their help.

2. You might be wondering how to identify isolated changes from those that can cascade though your website.

Changes to a style sheet are usually higher impact and not isolated. The problem is that it can be difficult to know which pages are using the style sheet.

Modifying the style sheet is high impact, since that change can cascade though the site. But adding elements to a style sheet are low impact, since nothing is using those new elements.

After any change to a style sheet, it's import to test the site and look for any breaking changes. Make changes slowly then test. Keep moving forward in that pattern.

Changes to a template are not isolated either. Any other pages using the template will be affected by the change. Following the above pattern of change slowly and test will help in identifying any broken areas.

3. Last is to apply a logical order to changes. Let's say you need to modify the home page, header and footer.

The homepage is a fairly isolated, low impact change. This would be a good place to start.

Next are the headers and footers. This possibly means changing a template, which is a higher impact change, affecting a larger portion of your site.

Depending on how complex the header and footer are, choose the one that seems as though it will be simpler to change then move on to the one that is more complex.

I say that because more complex changes will usually involve more time. While smaller changes provide quicker visual feedback and allow you to move forward.

The main point about applying any update to a live site is to have a plan and be prepared if anything goes wrong. Hopefully the above tips will help you.

Updates On Larger Websites

This section isn't going to be detailed. I wanted to mention how larger websites usually perform upgrades.

Often there is a staging area that any changes are promoted to. Once those changes have been thoroughly tested, they're promoted to the live site at some predetermined low traffic time.

This type of strict verification allows larger sites to make high impact changes but have high confidence that the site will not break once the changes go live.

Version control is also used, which provides an audit of code changes. This helps in rolling back any breaking changes.

While your site might not use such an elaborate upgrade strategy, I wanted you to at least be aware of other options. When the time comes, a more elaborate update strategy might be something for you to consider.

Chapter 15

Where Do You Go From Here?

We've covered a lot of ground. My goal was to arm you with an understanding of what a responsive web design is, when it should be used, its associated costs, and a summary of its technical aspects.

If that is all you wanted to understand about responsive web design, I hope you can now say, "Goal accomplished!"

For the more ambitious, who want to design a responsive website, I've put together a set of skills you'll need:

1. Practical knowledge in CSS and HTML
2. Ability to use browser debugging tools
3. Understanding of breakpoints

4. Ability to transform various elements into responsive layouts

The above doesn't require you to be an expert. It doesn't require you to spend hundreds or thousands of dollars on courses. You don't need to invest weeks or months to learn the above techniques.

Seeing someone walk through the building of a responsive web design from start to finish, watching him or her handle difficult situations, and understanding the reasoning behind various steps is all you need.

I'd like to help you reach this level and shortcut the learning process.

Beyond The Basics

"Practical Responsive Web Design" will help you accomplish all of the above without having to invest weeks or months of time. It will do it without you having to spend hundreds or thousands of dollars.

In the course, we'll start by building a solid foundation. From there, you'll see, step by step, how to create a responsive web design. You'll even discover how to transform an existing website into a responsive website.

The Next Step

You've already taken the first step by getting a great introduction to responsive web design.

Now it's time to take the next step. I want you to feel the satisfaction you'll get once you create your first responsive website.

Here's my special offer:

44% off
"Practical Responsive Web Design Introduction"

Just visit bitesizebschool.com/begin30 and you'll be on your way to gaining a rare, desirable skillset.

Thank you,
Brett Romero